XF-92

Convair's Arrow

Hugh Harkins

Copyright © 2013 Hugh Harkins

All rights reserved.

ISBN: 1-903630-53-3
ISBN-13: 978-1-903630-53-2

Research & Development Aircraft No.6

XF-92

CONVAIR'S ARROW

© Hugh Harkins 2013

Published by Centurion Publishing
United Kingdom

ISBN 10: 1-903630-53-3
ISBN 13: 978-1-903630-53-2

This volume first published in 2013

The Author is identified as the copyright holder of this work under sections 77 and 78 of the Copyright Designs and Patents Act 1988

Page layout, concept and design © Centurion Publishing

All rights reserved. No part of this publication may be reproduced, stored in a retrieval system, transmitted in any form, or by any means, electronic, mechanical or photocopied, recorded or otherwise, without the written permission of the Publishers

The Publishers and Author would like to thank all organizations and services for their assistance and contributions in the preparation of this publication, including the USAF and particularly NASA, whose many research documents and diagrams made this volume possible

Introduction

The Consolidated Vultee XP-92 was conceived as a Mach 1 plus point defence interceptor for the USAAF. It was initially planned to have a mixed rocket/turbojet power plant, but was cancelled by the new USAF. However, a single aircraft was built as the XF-92A research aircraft, which served with the USAF before being passed to NACA; being incorporated into that organizations High Speed Research Fleet. Although not attaining operational service, the XF-92A was a pioneering high speed delta wing flight research aircraft, paving the way for later delta wing interceptors and bombers such as the Convair F-012, F-106 and the supersonic B-58

CONTENTS

	Introduction	iv
1	CONVAIR XF-92A	1
2	XF-92A TESTING WITH NACA	19
3	APPENDICES	31
4	GLOSSARY	33

1

CONVAIR XF-92A

The single XF-92A during an early test flight. USAF

The XF-92A began life as the Convair Model 7002, which was developed using delta-wing technology pioneered by Dr Alexander Lippisch in Germany during the 1930's. After World War II Dr Lippisch's work was instrumental in development of the diverse Convair delta family of aircraft, of which the Model 7002 was the pioneer. In August 1945, the USAAF (United States Army Air Force) announced its wish for a jet powered interceptor capable of attaining 700-mph and reaching an altitude of 50,000-ft in four minutes; a tall order considering that the fastest jet powered fighter then flying was the British Gloster Meteor IV, which would eventually have am operational maximum speed of 585 mph, although two Meteor IV's were used to extend the World absolute speed record to 606 mph in November 1945.

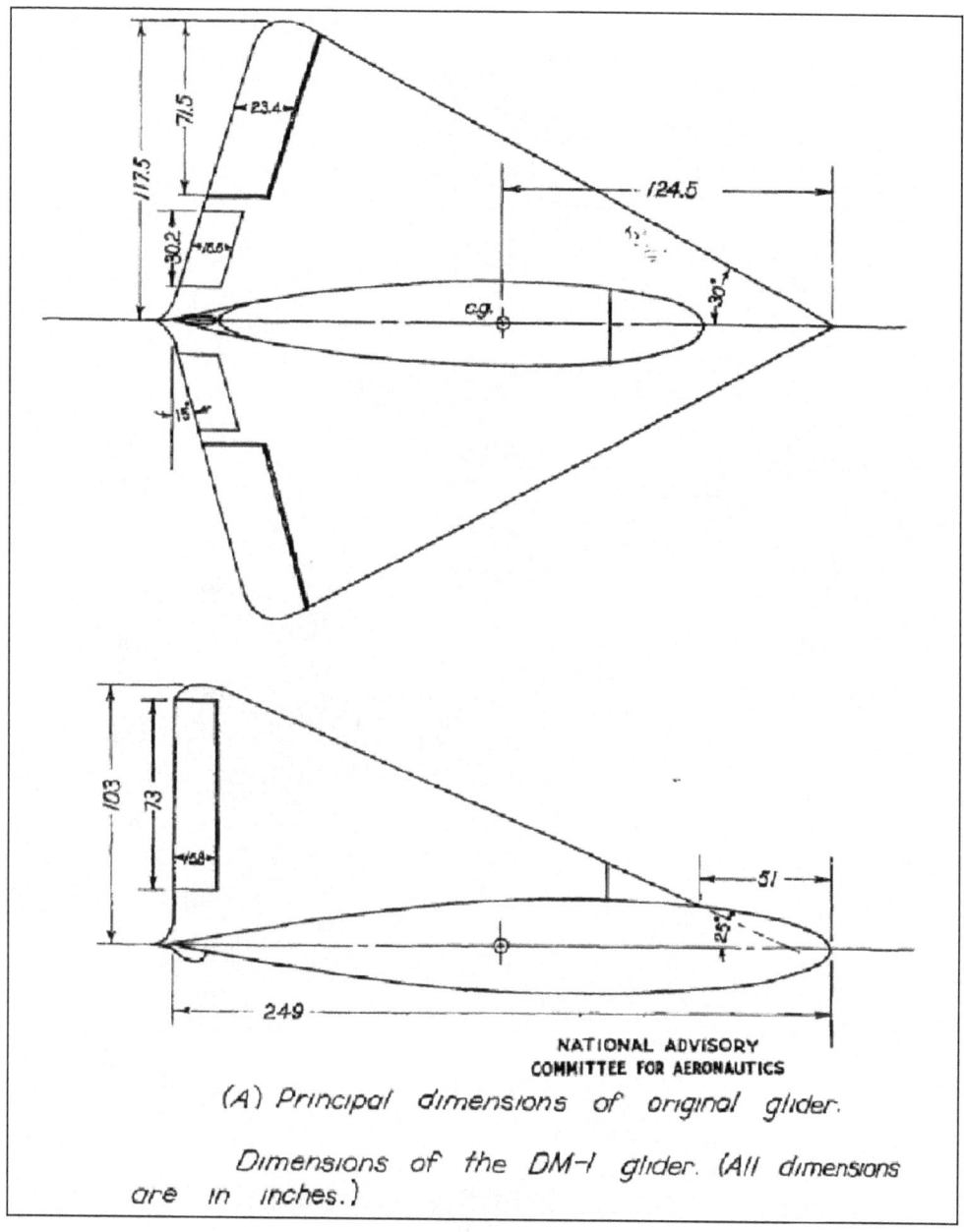

(A) Principal dimensions of original glider.

Dimensions of the DM-1 glider. (All dimensions are in inches.)

Previous page: The DM-1 delta research glider on an airfield occupied by the Allies at the end of the war in Europe in summer 1945. Above: The glider was transferred to the United States, where studies and testing, including wind-tunnel testing, were conducted by NACA. This 3-view general arrangement drawing shows the main dimensions of the unaltered DM-1 glider. Research data gleaned from programs like the DM-1 were incorporated into the XP-92 program. NASA

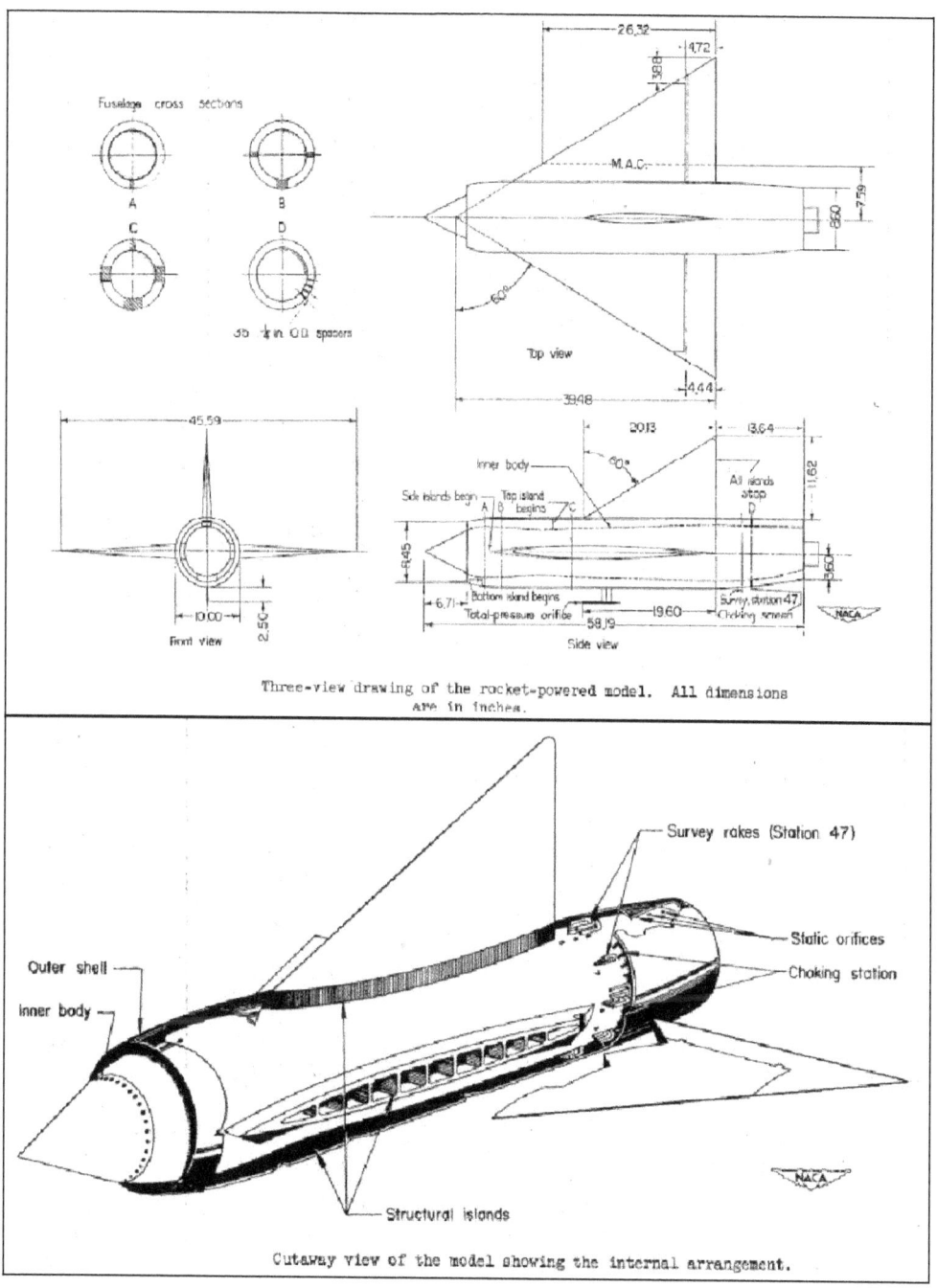

Three-view drawing of the rocket-powered model. All dimensions are in inches.

Cutaway view of the model showing the internal arrangement.

Previous page and this page: NACA conducted tests on a 1-8.25 scale model of the proposed XP-92 (XF-92) interceptor, with the main purpose of gaining data on the original inlet configuration. While the inlet was designed for high supersonic speeds, the tests investigated transonic and low supersonic characteristics. NASA

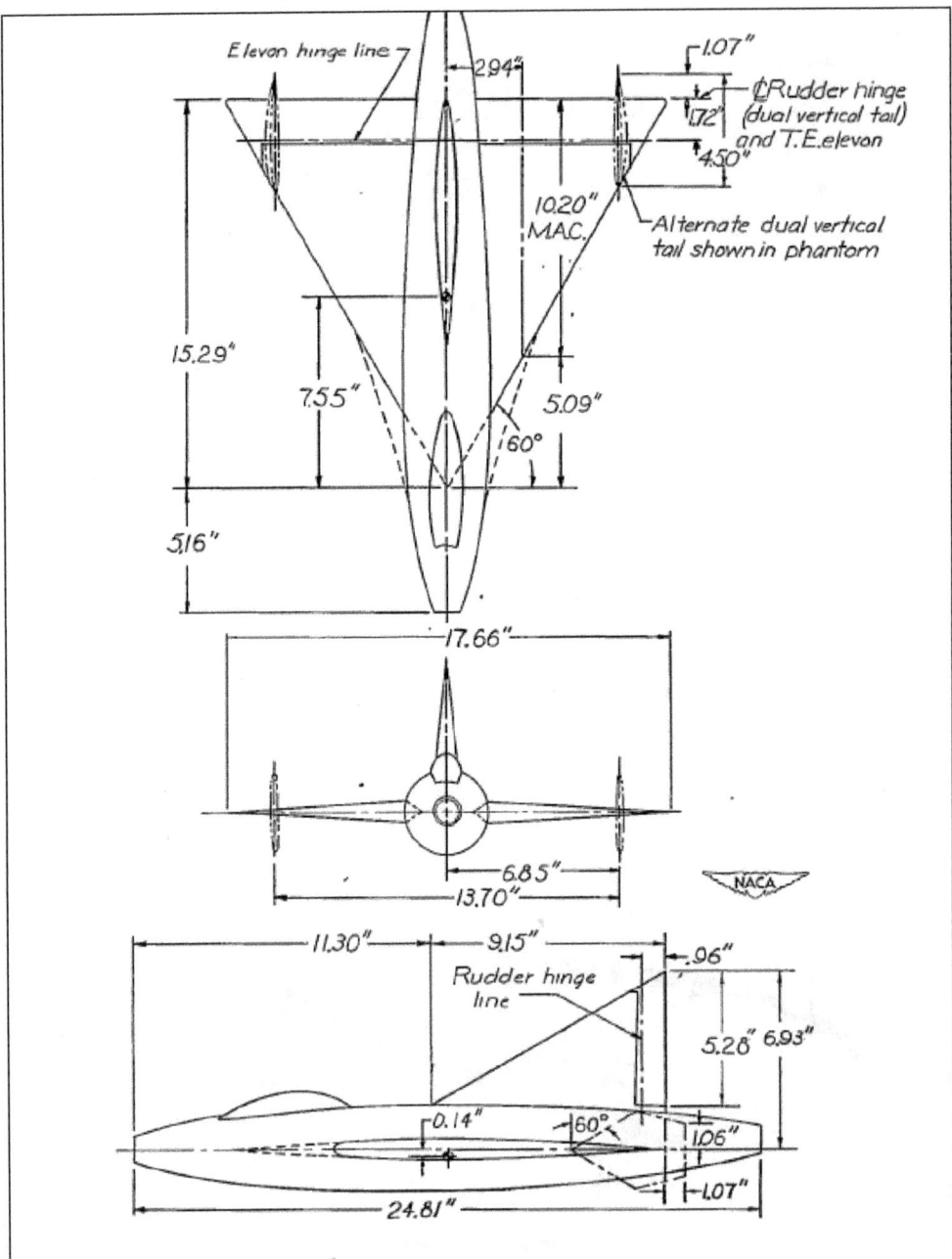

Drawing of a $\frac{1}{20}$-scale model of the Consolidated Vultee MX-813 airplane as tested in the free-spinning tunnel. Center of gravity is shown for the design gross weight loading.

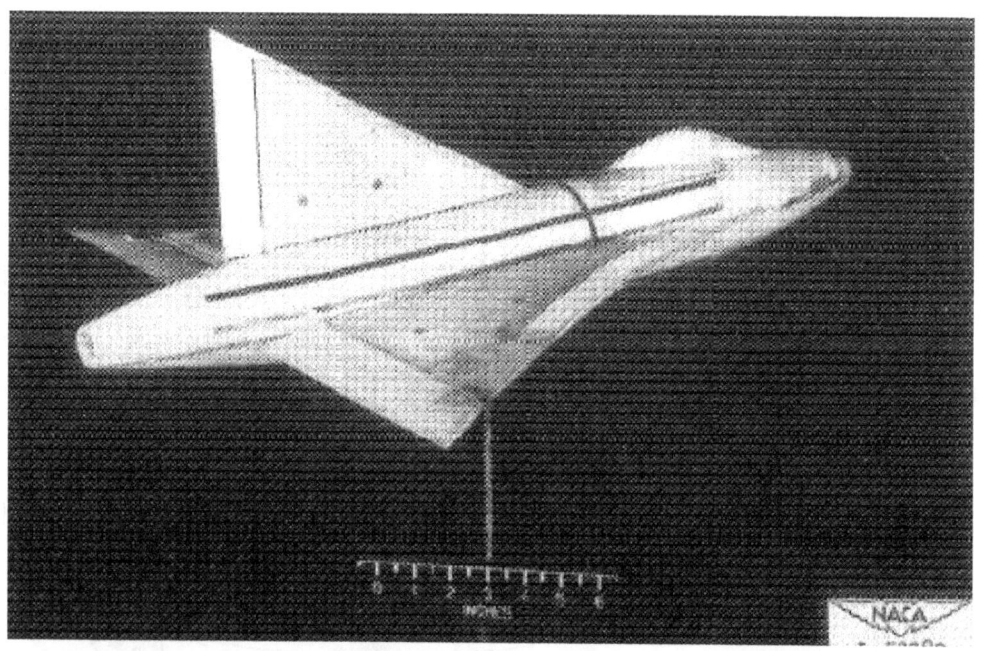

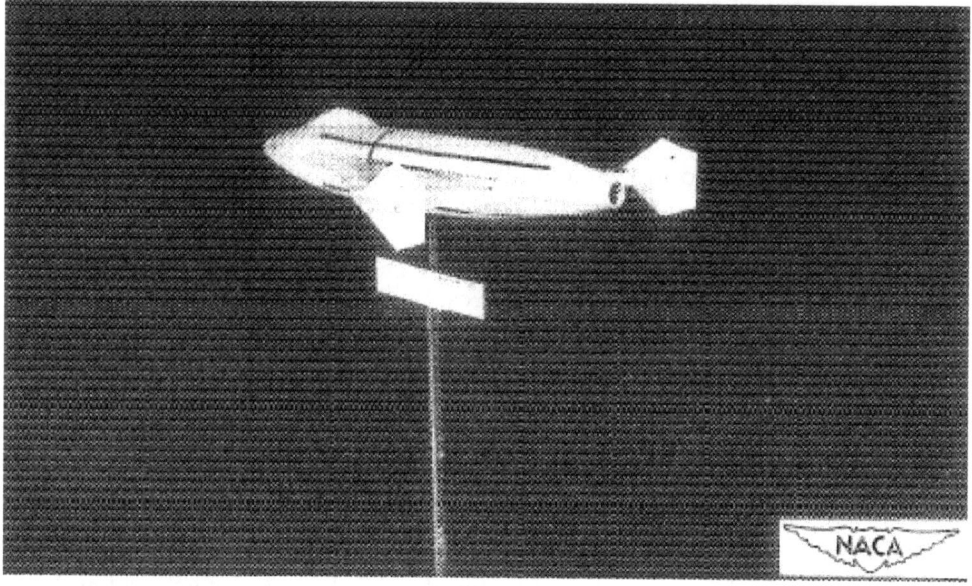

Top: Single vertical tail configuration of the 1-20th model of the Vultee MX-813. Above: The duel vertical tail configuration of the 1-20th model of the MX-813 being tested in a NACA wind-tunnel. NASA

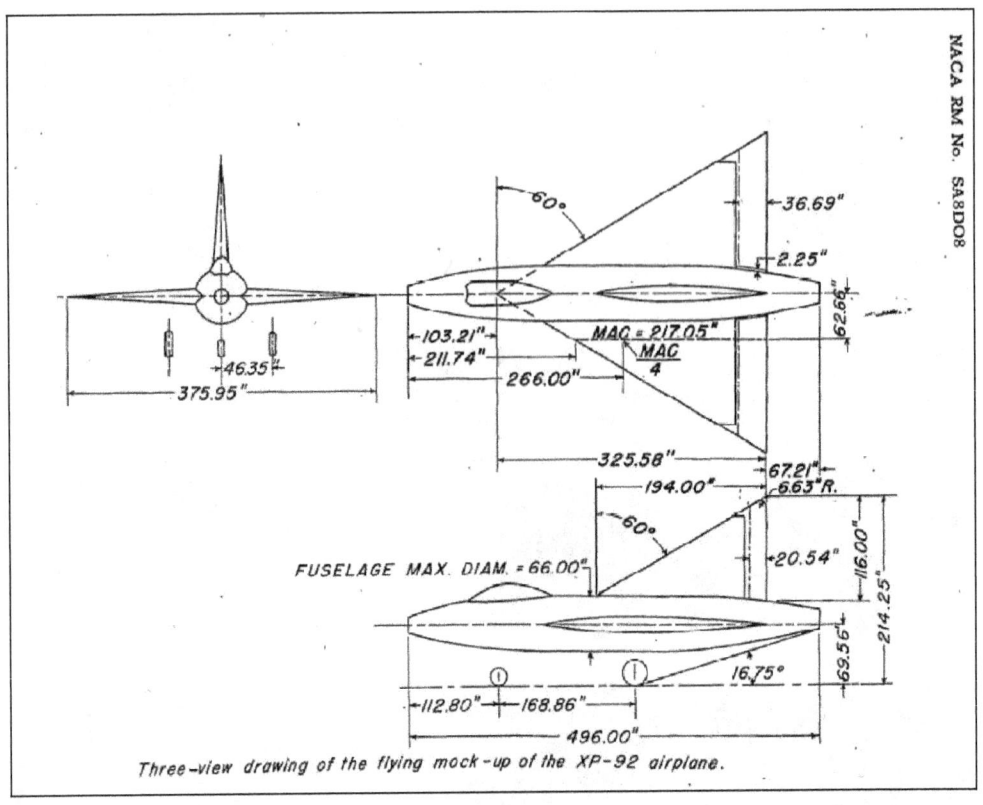

Three-view drawing of the flying mock-up of the XP-92 airplane.

In May 1946, the Consolidated Vultee (Convair) proposal for an interceptor, MX-813, to be designated P-92, was selected as the USAAF choice for further development. The initial P-92 proposal was for a ramjet powered aircraft with wings swept back at an angle of 45-degrees, building on German wartime swept wing data, although the aircraft as built would have a sweep-back of 60-degrees.

While the design was being refined on the drawing board wind tunnel testing revealed problems with wing tip stalling when flying at low-angle-of-attack, and lateral control problems. Going back to the drawing board, Convair decided to adapt the design to incorporate a delta wing using German research data, pioneered by Dr Alexander Lippisch, captured at the end of the war in Europe in 1945. The new delta wing design featured a 'V' shaped butterfly tail and was to be powered by a single Westinghouse J30-WE-1 turbojet engine rated at 1,560 lb static thrust, which would be augmented by up to six liquid fuelled rocket engines, each rated at 2,000-lb thrust. The aim was to produce an extremely fast point defense interceptor with an emphasis on out and out performance, with planned, unrealistic for the time, speeds of up to Mach 1.65. In short, this was an evolution of the German Me.263 rocket powered interceptor concept, albeit using a combination of jet and rocket power. The high performance was to be achieved at the expense of range, and the aircraft would have had an endurance of only 5.4-minutes.

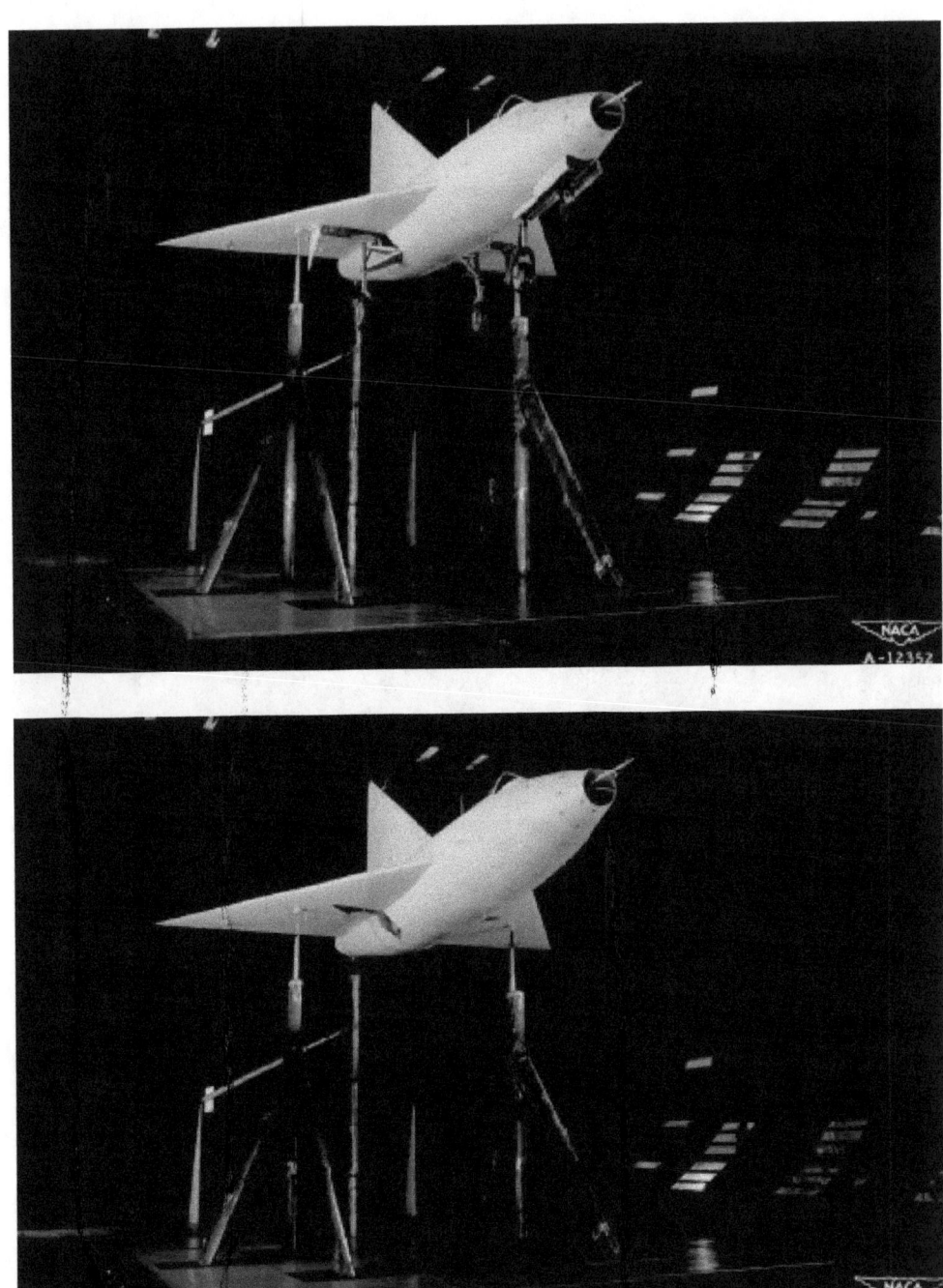

Previous page: The XP-92 FSM (Full Scale Mock-up) in Ames 40 x 80 ft wind tunnel. This page: The FSM in the tunnel with undercarriage extended and main doors removed (top) and undercarriage retracted and doors removed (bottom). NASA

The XF-92A on Muroc dry lake bed in natural metal finish after delivery to the USAF. USAF

At the time little was known about delta wing flight characteristics, therefore, in November 1946 the USAAF authorised Convair to build a research vehicle designated Model 7002 (7-002) as a 'flying mock-up' to investigate delta-wing behaviour at low and high subsonic speeds in support of the planned P-92 interceptor.

The single Model 7002, which was allocated the USAAF serial number (S/N) 46-682, featured a single tall vertical tail surface (a 'V' tail was planned for the P-92), which combined with the delta-wing plan-form gave the aircraft a distinctive, easily recognisable appearance. Air was fed to the engines through a relatively simple nose mounted air intake, similar to the types found in the earliest jet powered aircraft like the German Heinkel 178 and the British Gloster E.28/39 'Pioneer', which flew in 1939 and 1941 respectively.

To speed the program and reduce costs, the Model 7002 was built using a number of components from other aircraft. The hydraulic system and engine were taken from the Lockheed P-80 Shooting Star jet fighter; rudder pedals were taken from a BT-13 trainer aircraft; the main undercarriage came from the North American FJ-1 Fury naval jet fighter; the nose wheel came from the Bell P-63 Kingcobra piston engine fighter, and the ejector seat and cockpit canopy were taken from the Convair XP-81 mixed power plant jet/piston (planned to be fitted with a turboprop, but flew with a piston engine). The new delta wing plan-form required 'elevons' to be developed for the aircraft in place of the traditional aircraft wing elevators and ailerons. All of the aircraft's flight-controls were hydraulically actuated and irreversible.

This late 1940's Convair photograph shows the XF-92A alongside the nose section of a Convair B-36 Strategic Bomber.

Construction of the Model 7002 commenced at Vultee Field, California, however, when this site was closed down in mid-1947 the unfinished airframe was transferred to Convair's San Diego, California facility where construction was completed in autumn that year. The aircraft, without an engine, was moved to the NACA Ames aeronautical Laboratory at Moffat Field, California, for wind tunnel testing in December 1947, following which it was returned to San Diego for installation of an Allison J33-A-21 engine rated at 4,250-lb.

The Allison J33 turbojet engine that powered the aircraft was a development of General Electric J33, which powered the Lockheed P-80 Shooting Star jet fighter. This engine was directly developed from the British Whittle engines delivered to the United States in 1942/43. The first of the Americanised engines, designated J33, conducted static ground rig engine runs on 13 January 1944, and a variant flew in the XP-80 in June that year; this unit replacing the de

Havilland H-1A, which had previously been fitted in the XP-80. The J33 was used to power the production variants of the P-80 (later F-80), with responsibility for development and production of the engine being passed over to the Allison Division of General Motors from November 1945.

The XF-92A on the Dry Lake Bed at Muroc; still in natural metal finish. USAF

The XF-92A had a fleeting shot at movie stardom, being painted up as a fictional Soviet fighter dubbed the MiG-23 for the film 'Jet Pilot'. USAF

The XF-92A on the ramp at Muroc during USAF testing in 1952. USAF

In April 1948, the aircraft was moved to Muroc Dry Lake for testing, which was initially restricted to taxiing, high and slow speed runs, and ground testing, although a short hop off the Lake Bed was recorded on 9 June 1948.

While the Model 7002 was being prepared for flight-testing the USAF (previously USAAF; changed to USAF as a separate entity from the US Army in 1947) realised that the P-92 (F-92) point-defence interceptor was not a practical proposal for its interceptor aircraft requirements; with the propulsion system in particular proving to be impractical. This led to the programs cancellation in 1948. However, the delta-wing research continued as the Model 7002 was almost ready for flight-testing and the USAF was still interested in gaining additional data on delta-wing research for possible future military aircraft programs.

An Allison J33-A-23 turbojet engine, rated at 5,200-lb thrust, was installed before the aircraft's official first flight, which took place at Muroc Dry Lake (now Edwards AFB) on 18 September 1948, being hailed as the first true powered delta-wing aircraft to fly. The initial flight-test phase, which was completed by 26 August 1949, showed the controls to be extremely sensitive; the aircraft requiring good piloting skills to handle. This early flight test phase was conducted by Convair test pilots Sam Shannon and Bill Martin before the aircraft was handed over to the USAF for flight testing.

The XF-92A, resplendent in its overall white colour scheme, at Muroc (Edwards AFB) in June 1952. USAF

The Model 7002 was delivered to the USAF on 14 May 1949, at which time the aircraft was formally designated XF-92A, although it was a different aircraft from the planned XP-92 rocket interceptor, and it was clear that there was no possibility of a production contract for an operational aircraft. Following completion of the Phase 1 flight-testing the XF-92A underwent a test phase with USAF test pilots which showed that the aircraft performed well during landing and was stable at speeds up to Mach 0.92, but simply could not exceed the speed of sound in level flight and was only just capable of exceeding Mach 1.0 in a dive, which was done on at least one occasion (Major Frank K. "Pete" Everest was at the controls for this flight). The USAF test pilot phase of flight-test was completed at the end of 1949, with pilots, Captain Charles E. (Chuck) Yeager (the first recorded pilot to break the sound barrier in the Bell X-1 rocket powered aircraft), and Major Everest conducting most XF-92A flights.

Research continued, and in 1951 the aircraft was fitted with a J33-A-29 turbojet, which featured an afterburner nozzle, increasing thrust to 7,500-lb, although performance of the aircraft improved only marginally and the engine was fraught with maintenance problems resulting in only 21 flights (some documentation records 19 flights) being conducted over 19 months following fitment of the engine. The first of these flights with the re-engined XF-92A was conducted on 20 July 1951 with Yeager at the controls.

XF-92A

Previous page and this page: The XF-92A at the National Museum of the United States Air Force, where it resides in 2013. USAF

2

XF-92A TESTING WITH NACA

The XF-92A was delivered to NACA following its retirement from testing by the USAF. The aircraft is shown outside the HSFRS hanger at Muroc. NASA

Dissatisfaction with the J33-A-29 engine saw it replaced by a J33-A-16 rated at 8,400-lb thrust, which powered the aircraft when it commenced a flight-test program with NACA beginning on 9 April 1953, with NACA test pilot Scott Crossfield at the controls. NACA immediately grasped the opportunity of incorporating the XF-92A into its test fleet, mainly because its delta wing configuration translated into large wing area, and because of the "thin airfoil cross section and low aspect ratio". Prior to the XF-92's first flight, and several years before it would incorporate the aircraft into its test fleet, NACA had conducted many test programs with the aircraft, particularly in the low-speed wind-tunnel at its Ames Centre.

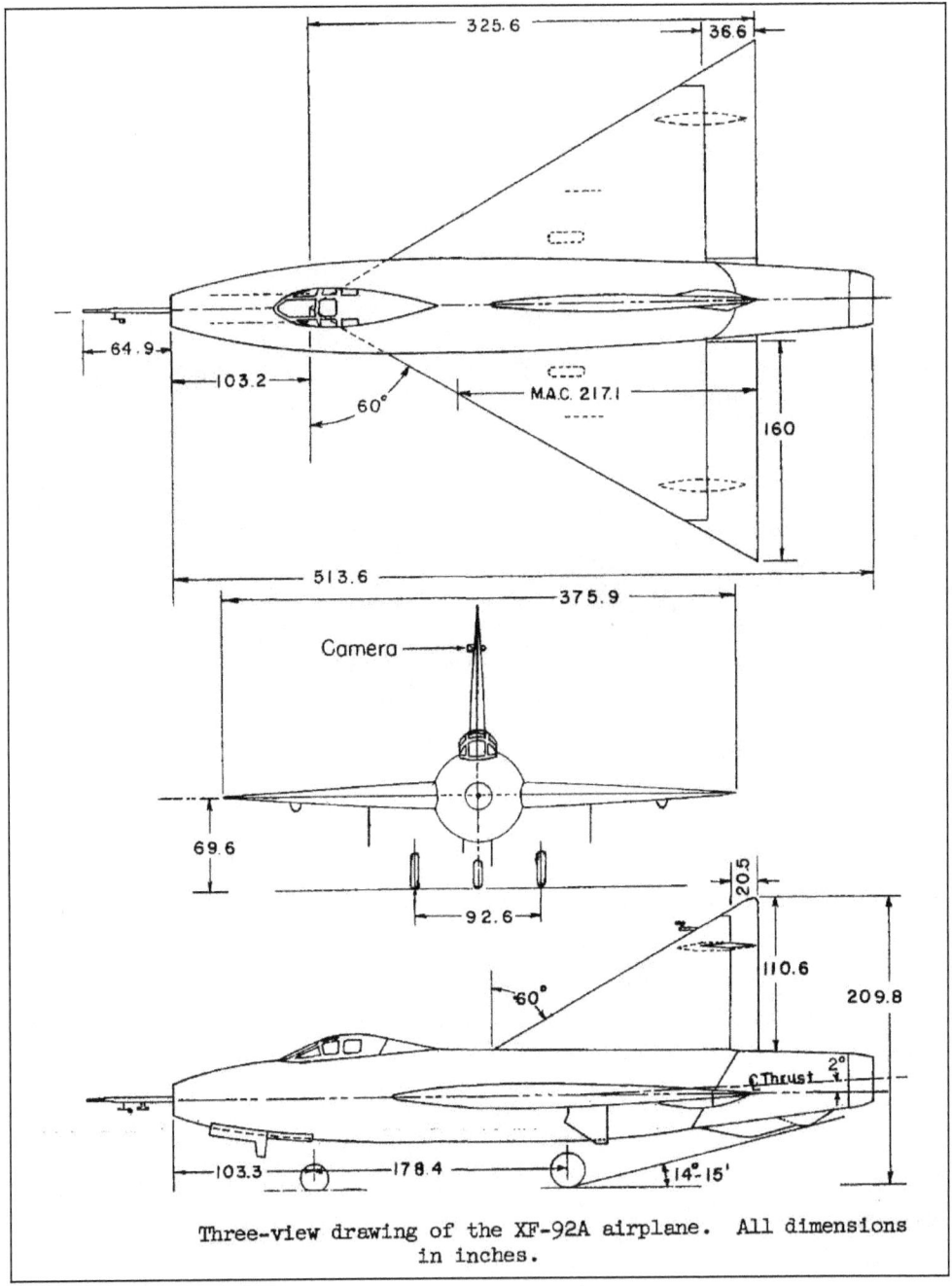

Three-view drawing of the XF-92A airplane. All dimensions in inches.

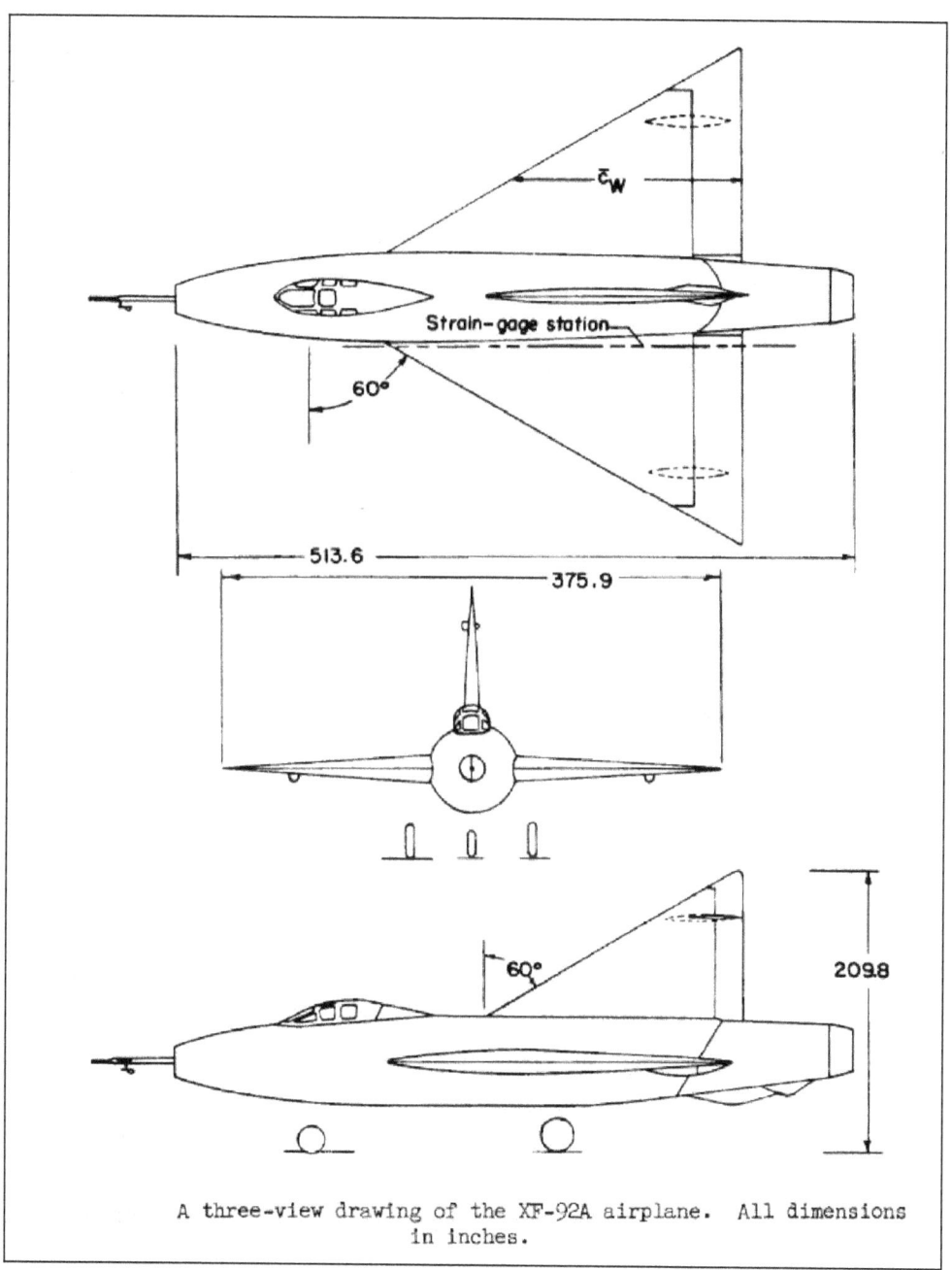

A three-view drawing of the XF-92A airplane. All dimensions in inches.

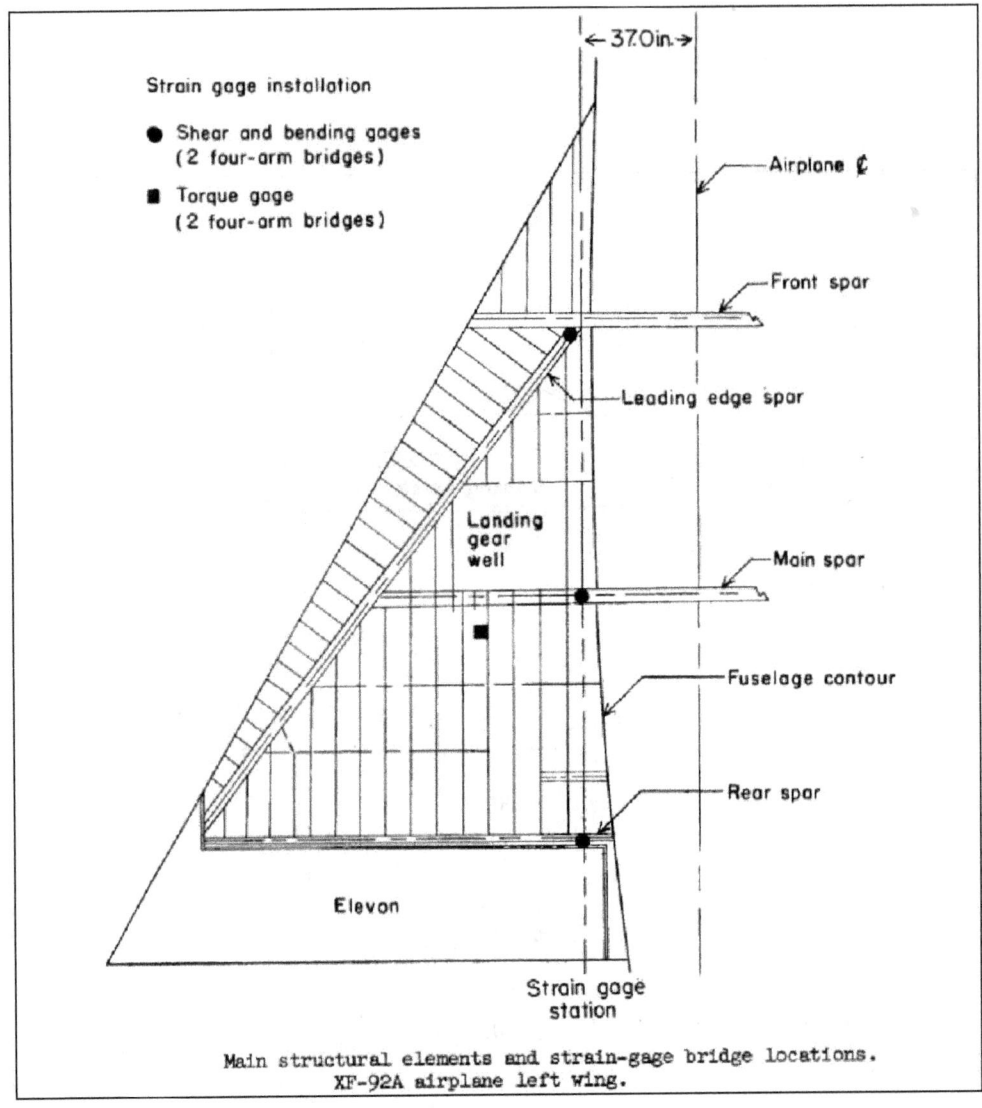

Main structural elements and strain-gage bridge locations.
XF-92A airplane left wing.

With NACA, the XF-92A was not a stand-alone research program, the aircraft being integrated into the wider supersonic, transonic flight research program. In 1949, NACA had been offered the original X-1 (previously XS-1; the XS-1 and XS-2 were re-designated X-1 and X-2 on 11 June 1948) as a research tool. However, this was declined. NACA had its own ideas of what kind of aircraft it required for the new phase of supersonic/transonic flight research beyond the original X-1 and Bell D-558-1 programs; these included the Douglas X-3 Stiletto, Northrop X-4 Bantam, Bell X-5, Convair XF-92A, advanced variants of the Bell X-1, and the rocket powered Douglas D-558-2 and Bell X-2.

These aircraft would be operated by the NACA HSFRS (High Speed Flight Research Station) now the Dryden Flight Research Centre, Edwards AFB. The HSFRS research approach included studies into aerodynamic configuration, stability and control, and handling qualities. For "five basic configurations; the sweptwing, the semitailless, the delta wing, the variable sweep wing, and the low aspect ratio thin wing", all of which were tested.

The following, is reproduced from NASA (NACA) publications:

Configuration	Aircraft	Speed Range
Swept-wing	Douglas D-558-2 #3	Mach 1.0
Semi-tailless	Northrop X-4 #2	Mach 0.9
Delta Wing	Convair XF-92A	Mach 0.9+
Variable-sweep	Bell X-5 #1	Mach 0.9+
Low AR thin wing	Douglas X-3	Mach 0.95

The above mentioned aircraft were also involved in investigating "aerodynamic or dynamic stability problems" as follows:

Aircraft	Research Problem
Douglas D-558-2 #3	Sweptwing pitch-up during maneuvering.
Northrop X-4 #2	Pitching oscillation of increasing severity approaching mach 0.95.
Convair XF-92A	Delta pitch-up during maneuvering
Bell X-5 #1	Unacceptable stall-spin behavior: sweptwing pitch-up during maneuvering
Douglas X-3	Coupled motion instability during abrupt rolling maneuvers

From the upper frontal aspect the XF-92A took on an almost arrowhead appearance. NASA

This test-phase showed the XF-92A aircraft had a tendency to pitch-up violently during high-speed turns. Modifications to the aircraft saw wing fences fitted, which improved things slightly, but the problem remained. This problem was not unique to the XF-92A within the HSFRS fleet. All of the aircraft being tested, with the exception of the X-3, exhibited the pitch-up problem. Of all the aircraft in the HSFRS fleet only the D-558-2 was considered to have "pleasant flying characteristics", the others, including the XF-92A, leaving much to be desired. The XF-92A was considered to be "Sluggish and underpowered", a problem which also plagued the X-3, while the X-4 exhibited "Poorly damped 'Hunting' motion about all three axes: 'washboard road' motion", and the X-5 exhibited "Dangerous stall approach and spin tendencies". So violent were the XF-92A's 'pitch-up' tendencies during turns that it often exceeded 6 g and on at least one occasion exceeded 8 g.

The XF-92A was part of a wider program involving a number of aircraft operated by the NACA HSFRS. Here the aircraft is shown with other elements of that fleet. From left to right: Bell X-1A, D-558-1, XF-92A, X-4, D-558-2, X-4 and the X-3 in the centre. NASA

Previous page: The XF-92A outside the HSFRS hanger (top) and on the ramp at Muroc (bottom). Above: The XF-92A (centre right) in the maintenance hangar at Muroc (Edwards) along with an assortment of other aircraft including an YF-84, D-558-1, D-558-2 and B-47 L-R. NASA

Basically 'pitch-up' was a term used to describe a problem encountered by swept wing (including delta) aircraft as they approached flight conditions that would bring about a stall; at low speed when the aircraft was flown at "increasingly higher nose up angles of attack" or at increasingly lower speeds, or when flying at high speed during "an abrupt turning maneuver at a high-g loading", in this case, naturally the airflow circulating around the aircraft's wing " is accentuated, notably the tendency of the airflow to flow outward toward the wing tips (spanwise flow), promoting the development of so called 'separated' airflow, causing a loss of lift at the wing tips. As the stall condition progresses, the area of the stall moves progressively 'up' the wing toward the wing root, followed by the centre of lift of the wing".

The XF-92A during a 1953 flight with NACA. NASA

There were several potential fixes to cure 'pitch-up' tendencies, such as a 'saw-tooth' leading-edge extension, which was effectively designed to create or enhance 'active' airflow, thereby eliminating or reducing the tendency of the wing to "exhibit spanwise flow". Another potential fix was the incorporation of 'wing-fences', which were basically just that; small fences "running in a chordwise flow". 'Open wing-slats' were developed from technology going back to the 1920's; effectively designed to postpone "the onset of turbulent airflow over the wing at high angles of attack".

All of the above mentioned fixes were flight tested on the Douglass D-558-2 and the XF-92A (the XF-92A was fitted with wing-fences planned for the Convair F-102 Delta Dart interceptor being developed for the USAF as this aircraft, in its original form, had adopted a similar wing plan-form to the XF-92A), contributing to the design characteristics of the first generation of US supersonic fighters, typified by the North American F-100 Super Sabre and the Vought F8U Crusader, both of which adopted low set tail-planes, which testing of the pitch-up tendencies of the aircraft at the HSFRS had shown to be desirable in reducing 'pitch-up tendencies. Other supersonic fighters being designed at the time such as the McDonnell F-101 Voodoo entered service plagued with severe "mission limiting pitch-up characteristics". Testing with the HSFRS fleet, including the XF-92A, had shown that having the "horizontal tail low on the aft fuselage of an aircraft where it would be below the wing wake and downwash of the wing" was considered the best solution to reducing 'pitch-up' characteristics. Of course, in the case of the XF-92A there was a complete absence of horizontal tail-planes.

The following table from a NASA (NACA) publication shows the duration and number of flights conducted by the five aircraft types initially employed by the HSFRS:

Aircraft	Number of Flights	Duration of NACA Tests
Douglas D-558-2 #3	66	1950-1956
Northrop X-4 #2	82	1950-1953
Convair XF-92A	25	1953
Bell X-5 #1	113	1952-1955
Douglas X-3	20	1954-1956

The XF-92A was scheduled for more flight tests, but was retired following an accident on its 25th NACA flight on 14 October 1953.

On 14 October 1953, the single XF-92A was damaged when the nose-gear collapsed during a landing (documentation differs as to the aircraft duties at the time of the accident, both landing rollout and a high speed taxi run being put forward) bringing the aircrafts flight career to an abrupt end. However, the XF-92A had performed sterling work in the research into delta wing flight, in particular gaining valuable data showing that the stability and control characteristics of the delta wing concept was sound and practical for incorporation into high performance aircraft. This research data proved invaluable in future programs including the Convair/USAF Project 1554 known as the 1954 interceptor because of the original planned in service date, which was won by the Convair F-102 Delta Dagger; which was essentially developed from the XF-92A, the later Convair F-106 Delta Dart interceptor, and the same companies much larger B-58 supersonic bomber and XF2Y-1 Sea Dart.

Following a period of outside storage the XF-92A was incorporated as an education tool and in 1969 the aircraft was transferred from the University of South Sewanee to the USAF Museum at Wright Paterson AFB, Ohio where it remained in 2013.

XF-92A NACA Flights (NASA)

Flight #	Flight Date	Duty
1	9.4.1953	Pilot check; static longitudinal stability investigation.
2	16.4.1953	Static and dynamic stability and control.
3	21.4.1953	Longitudinal Stability and control.
4	27.5.1953	Longitudinal Stability and control.
5	3.6.1953	Longitudinal Stability and control.
6	5.6.1953	Longitudinal Stability and control.
7	9.6.1953	Longitudinal Stability and control.
8	11.6.1953	Longitudinal Stability and control.
9	16.6.1953	Longitudinal Stability and control.
10	19.6.1953	Longitudinal Stability and control.
11	24.6.1953	Longitudinal Stability and control.
12	24.6.1953	Longitudinal Stability and control.
13	26.6.1953	Low-speed Stability and control.
14	3.7.1953	First flight with wing fences.
15	3.7.1953	Second fence flight.
16	22.7.1953	Modified fence design; fences buckled in flight.
17	17.8.1953	Engine malfunctioned, aborted flight.
18	20.8.1953	Longitudinal Stability and control with modified fence design
19	20.8.1953	Same as flight 18.
20	30.9.1953	Low-speed lateral and directional control with fences.
21	30.9.1953	Same as flight 20.
22	2.10.1953	Same as flight 20.
23	5.10.1953	Same as flight 20.
24	14.10.1953	Low-speed lateral and directional control without fences.
25	14.10.1953	Same as flight 24. Nose landing gear collapsed during landing rollout. Plane was retired.

APPENDICES

Appendix I

Variants

XP-92: Convair Model 7002, none built
XF-92A: 1 aircraft built as a delta-wing research aircraft

Appendix II

Specification

XF-92A

Engines: One Allison J33-A-29 rated at 7,500-lb with afterburner
Length: 42-ft 6-in
Height: 17-ft 9-in
Wingspan: 31-ft 4-in
Weights: 14,608-lb maximum take-off
Maximum speed: Mach 0.9+
Cruising speed: 655-mph
Service ceiling: 50,750-ft (other figures quoted are 40,000-ft)
Range: N/A
Armament: No armament
Crew: One

Appendix III

Specification Allison J33-A-35 (used in the F-80C); similar, but lower power than the later variants used in the J33-A-29 and J33-A-16 using afterburner
Compressor: Single stage centrifugal
Turbine: Single axial
Weight: 1,795 lb
Thrust: 4,600 lb
Maximum RPM: 11,750
Maximum operating altitude: 47,000 ft

Appendix IV

TABLE I.- PHYSICAL CHARACTERISTICS OF THE XF-92A AIRPLANE

Wing:
- Area, sq ft 425
- Span, ft 31.33
- Airfoil section . . . . NACA $65_{(06)}$-006.5
- Wing-panel area, outboard of root strain-gage station, sq ft 137.1
- Mean aerodynamic chord, ft 18.09
- Aspect ratio 2.31
- Root chord, ft 27.13
- Tip chord 0
- Taper ratio 0
- Sweepback (leading edge), deg 60
- Incidence, deg 0
- Dihedral (chord plane), deg 0

Elevons:
- Area (total, both, aft of hinge line) sq ft 76.19
- Span (one elevon), ft 13.35
- Chord (aft of hinge line, constant except at tip), ft 3.05
- Movement, deg
  - Elevator:
    - Up 15
    - Down 5
  - Aileron, total 10
- Operation . . . . Hydraulic

Vertical tail:
- Area, sq ft 75.35
- Height, above fuselage center line, ft 11.50

Rudder:
- Area, sq ft 15.53
- Span, ft 9.22
- Travel, deg . . . . ±8.5
- Operation . . . . Hydraulic

Fuselage:
- Length, ft 42.80

Power plant:
- Engine . . . . Allison J33-A-29 with afterburner
- Rating:
  - Static thrust at sea level, lb 5,600
  - Static thrust at sea level with afterburner, lb 7,500

Weight:
- Gross weight (560 gal fuel), lb 15,560
- Empty weight, lb 11,808

Center-of-gravity locations:
- Gross weight (560 gal fuel), percent M.A.C. 25.5
- Empty weight, percent M.A.C. 29.2
- Moment of inertia in pitch, slug-ft^2 35,000

Wing-panel weight, lb:
- Right 973
- Left 1,089

NASA

GLOSSARY

AR	Aspect Ratio
B	Bomber
Convair	Consolidated Vultee
F	Fighter
ft	Feet
HSFRS	High Speed Flight Research Station
MPH	Miles Per Hour
NACA	National Advisory Committee for Aeronautics
NASA	National Air and Space Administration
P	Pursuit
RPM	Revolutions Per Minute
S/N	Serial Number
US	United States
USAAF	United States Army Air Force
USAF	United States Air Force
X	Experimental
XF	Experimental Fighter
XP	Experimental Pursuit

ABOUT THE AUTHOR

Hugh, a Historian and author, has published in excess of thirty books; non-fiction and fiction, writing under his own name as well as utilising two different Pseudonyms. He has also written for several international magazines, while his work has been used as reference for many other projects ranging from the Aviation industry, international news corporations, film media to encyclopedias and the computer gaming industry. He currently resides in his native Scotland

www.ingramcontent.com/pod-product-compliance
Lightning Source LLC
Chambersburg PA
CBHW081024040426
42444CB00014B/3346